THIS BOOK IS LITERALLY JUST PICTURES OF CUTE ANIMALS THAT WILL MAKE YOU FEEL BETTER

Smith Street Books

Published in 2019 by Smith Street Books
Melbourne | Australia
smithstreetbooks.com

ISBN: 978-1-92581-118-6

CIP data is available from the National Library of Australia.

Publisher: Paul McNally
Design and layout: Hannah Koelmeyer
Cover photo: Retales Botijero / Getty Images
Image research: Hannah Koelmeyer and Patrick Boyle

Printed & bound in China by C&C Offset Printing Co., Ltd.

Book 96
10 9 8 7 6 5